ALL YOU WANTED TO KNOW ABOUT
Gem Therapy

GW00725968

VIJAYA KUMAR

New Dawn

NEW DAWN
a division of Sterling Publishers (P) Ltd.
A-59, Okhla Industrial Area, Phase-II, New Delhi-110020
Tel : 6313023, 6320118, 6916209, 6916165
E-mail : ghai@nde.vsnl.net.in
www.sterlingpublishers.com

All You Wanted to Know About - Gem Therapy
© 1999, Sterling Publishers Private Limited
ISBN 81 207 2195 0
Reprint 2001

All rights are reserved. No part of this publication may be
reproduced, stored in a retrieval system or transmitted, in any
form or by any means, mechanical, photocopying, recording
or otherwise, without prior written permission of the
publisher.

Published by Sterling Publishers Pvt. Ltd., New Delhi-110020.
Lasertypeset by Vikas Compographics, New Delhi-110020.
Printed at Sai Printers, New Delhi-110020.

Contents

Preface

This book is by no means an extensive study by any professional. The data provided in this book are my own interpretations of the subject, gleaned from various books, and presented from a layperson's viewpoint.

The book deals with each aspect of the study, point by point, in a simple language, and serves as a ready reckoner for those who have no time to go through heavy, indepth studies.

The publishers and I hold no responsibility for any discrepancy in the script. We would welcome suggestions or intimation of errors that come to anybody's notice.

Vijaya Kumar

Introduction

Our body is composed of cosmic radiations and seven colours — violet, indigo, blue, green, yellow, orange and red — which become imbalanced in course of time. Astral gems are carefully selected for use to affect the body beneficially through their measured radiations.

Gems increase the psychic powers of an individual, in addition to warding off the ill-effects of planets, by their curative powers.

A gem should be set in the right metal and with the right weight. It should be worn on the correct finger of the working hand on the right day. Each gem, with its constant source of a specific ray, gives rise to constructive vibrations that have therapeutic powers.

Gems — An Overview

1. All stones or gems have magnetic powers in varying degrees, and many of them are beneficial to us for their therapeutic cures.
2. They emit vibrations and frequencies which have strong potential influence on our whole being.
3. They create strong energy fields which enable us to be charged with their energies.

4. The gems are used for healing, transforming, balancing, and attuning the body, mind and soul.

5. They are a manifestation of vibrancy, light and colour, life, textures, transparency and clarity.

6. They activate our abilities, soothe and comfort, heal and balance through the purity of their rays.

7. The patterns in the stones reveal to us the changes that keep taking place, indicating that life is change — that the process of evolution is a cosmic law.

8. Each gem, tuned to a particular ray, has a special role to play.

9. The gems can be cleaned by leaving them under running water for six to eight hours. Or, bury them in some earth overnight, and rinse them off. Or, keep the stone in the flame of a candle till the candle melts. Or, else, place the stone amongst a heap of quartz for several days, whereby its energy is revived from the contact of the quartz.

10. The gem that is cleaned should be placed in direct sunlight, for the sun is a great source of energy and purification.

11. The quartz crystal, a catalyst and conductor of energy, balances and harmonises the aura.

12. As a force of light and energy, the quartz crystal protects against negative conditions in the aura of people of all ages, and cleanses the atmospheres of areas like our houses or work places.

13. The quartz crystal acts as a tranquilliser, and helps our intuitive insights by helping to see the light in the darkness.

14. The contact of the crystal quartz with the body helps in

dissolving the blocks that stem the flow of energy in our body.

15. Certain stones represent certain beliefs, which are as follows

Crystal — light

Turquoise — infinity of sea and sky

Coral — life and form

Gold — golden ray of the sun

Silver — the light of the moon

16. The more precious stones that you wear, the more strongly will you be charged with cosmic forces, radiating out into your surroundings.

17. Wear your stones — don't store them in a safe or a jewellery box,

for you will be depriving your body of this tremendous power bestowed upon us.

18. Stones serve both ways, cut or uncut, in healing. A cut and polished garnet is more beneficial than an uncut one, while the amethyst serves best in its crystal form.

19. Precious stones have potent magical properties, but alternative stones can be replaced if the cost factor is the stumbling block. The following stones can replace the precious stones.

Crystal quartz for diamonds
Garnets for rubies
Turquoise for aquamarine
Lapis-lazuli for blue sapphire
Carnelian for fire opal
Malachite for emeralds
Azurite for indigo sapphire

20. The precious stones have a way of healing emotions that have been inharmonious.

21. The stones selected for use should always be in contact with one's body to absorb their healing properties.

Gems and Zodiacal Signs

1. All gems are related to planetary forces, and anyone wearing jewels will be in harmony with his or her stellar rays.
2. The stones related to the zodiacal signs and colour rays are shown below:

Sign	Gems	Colour
Aries	Ruby, blood -stone, red jasper	Red
Taurus	Golden topaz, coral, emerald	Yellow

Gemini	Crystal, aquamarine	Violet
Cancer	Emerald, moonstone	Green
Leo	Ruby, amber	Orange
Virgo	Pink jasper, turquoise, zircon	Violet
Libra	Opal, diamond	Yellow
Scorpio	Garnet, topaz, agate	Red
Sagitta-rius	Amethyst	Purple

Capricorn	Smoky quartz, blue beryl, jet	Blue
Aquarius	Blue-sapphire	Indigo
Pisces	Diamond, jade, aquamarine	Indigo

3. Many people prefer to use stones that relate to their astrological sun sign. These sun signs are as follows:

Aries

The symbol of this sign is activity — initiative, ambition or creativity. Arians always rise from the lowest to the highest form — from red to white.

Gems : All red stones, like garnet, ruby, red jasper, are associated with Aries.

Taurus

The symbols of this sign are love and wisdom. Taureans are closely attuned to products of the earth.

They need to transform the love of personal to that of selfless service.

Gems : All yellow stones like topaz, citrine, amber are the gems of Taurus.

17

Gemini

This is the sign of duality. It symbolises life and death, joy and sorrow, health and sickness, plenty and poverty.

Gem : All violet stones, like amethyst or fluoride, are Geminian stones.

Cancer

This symbolises love and life. The magic power of love is the message and quest of this sign.

Gems : All green stones — emerald, jade, peridot, agate, green jasper — are the Cancerian stones.

Leo

This is the sign of wisdom and activity. Divinity and humility are keynotes for meditation for the native of this sign.

Gem : All gold and orange stones — amber, orange jasper, carnelian, fire opal, topaz — are associated with Leo.

Virgo

This symbolises reason which transforms to wisdom. Knowledge and understanding produce wisdom.

Gem : Amethyst and fluorite are the gems of this sign.

Libra

It symbolises the balance that must be weighed with the deeds of the year. It symbolises the unfolding of love which leads to unity.

Gem : Yellow stones — topaz, amber, citrine — are this sign's gems.

Scorpio

This is one of the most powerful signs. Its force being dual in aspect, it moves from the lowest depths to the greatest heights. It purifies the animal nature and lifts forces to a higher plane of expression.

Gem : Red and clear crimson stones — ruby, garnet, coral, red jasper, bloodstone — are the gems associated with this sign.

Sagittarius

This sign symbolises high idealism and noble aspirations. Its highest expression is a spiritualised mind.

Gem : Blue stones — sapphire, lapis-lazuli, blue topaz, sodalite — are linked with Sagittarius.

Capricorn

This sign denotes the mystery of the darkest night and the glory of the light. This sign symbolises the crossing of the bridge of darkness before reaching the radiation of the great white light. The goal for a Capricornian is to conquer one's ego.

Gem : Black and white stones — black tourmaline, jet, moonstone, opal, pearl — have significance for this sign.

Aquarius

This sign symbolises promotion of communication and group work. The goal of an Aquarian is to achieve oneness of the

whole, or wholeness of the one.
Gems : Clear blue stones — blue topaz, lapis-lazuli, sapphire — are the gems of this zodiacal sign.

Pisces

This sign symbolises selfless service which is the ideal way to achieve success. It denotes the spirit which struggles to rescue humanity from greed.

Gem : Soft blue and indigo stones — blue topaz, indigo sapphire, azurite — are a Piscean's ideal gems.

The Magical Influence of Planets

1. Electronic radiation from planets produce cellular change in human bodies.
2. The use of gems is recommended to mitigate the evil effects of certain planets in certain positions in the solar system.
3. The effect of a particular gem lasts so long as a particular planet wields its influence on one. Since planets are always in

transit, has to change one's stone according to the movement of the planets.

4. All gems, except red coral and ruby, should be soaked in raw milk for at least three hours to remove impurities; red coral in soap water, and ruby in lemon juice for three hours will remove impurities from them.

5. You may wish to work with a certain stones on a particular day, or wear one that represents the day of the week on which you were born.

The following table given below gives the gems for particular days of the week.

Day	Planetary Ruler	Gem
Sun.	Sun	Amber, Gold, Topaz
Mon.	Moon	Pearl, Moonstone
Tues.	Mars	Ruby, Garnet
Wed.	Mercury	Turquoise Sapphire, Lapis-lazuli
Thurs	Jupiter	Amethyst

| Fri. | Venus | Emerald, Malachite, Jade |
| Sat. | Saturn | Diamond, Smoky-quartz, Opal |

The planets associated with gems and zodiac signs are as follows :

Planet	Gem	Zodiac Sign Lord
Sun	Ruby	Leo
Moon	Pearl	Cancer
Mars	Coral	Aries, Scorpio

Mercury	Emerald	Gemini, Virgo
Jupiter	Topaz	Sagittarius, Pisces
Venus	Diamond	Taurus, Libra
Saturn	Sapphire	Capricorn, Aquarius
Rahu	Zircon	
Ketu	Cat's Eye	

6. Each finger, directly connected with a specific part of the body, is under the governance of a specific planet.

Index Finger

1. Jupiter controls this finger.
2. It relates to the respiratory system and the stomach.
3. Pearl, coral and topaz are recommended to be set in a ring and worn on this finger.
4. Moonstone and white pearl can also be worn to ensure sound sleep.

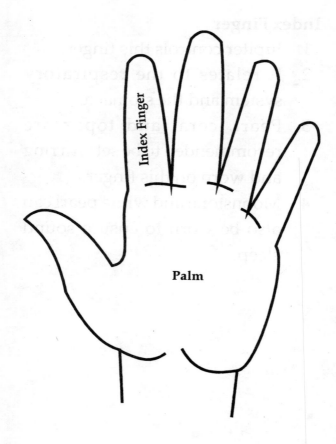

Middle Finger

1. Saturn rules this finger.
2. It represents intestines, mind, brain and liver.
3. Emerald, diamond and zircon are recommended.
4. Moonstone, sapphire, white coral and white pearl are also worn.

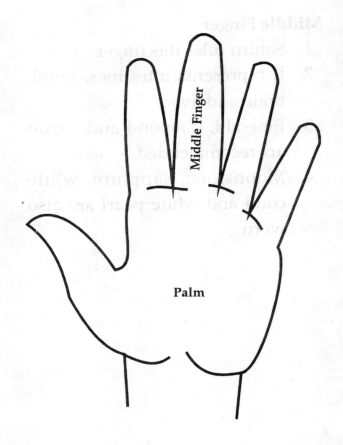

Middle Finger

Palm

Ring Finger

1. The ruling lord of this finger is Sun.
2. It is associated with kidneys, stomach, respiratory system, and blood circulation.
3. Coral, topaz and cat's eyes are beneficial gems.
4. Ruby, red coral, white pearl and moonstone can be worn.

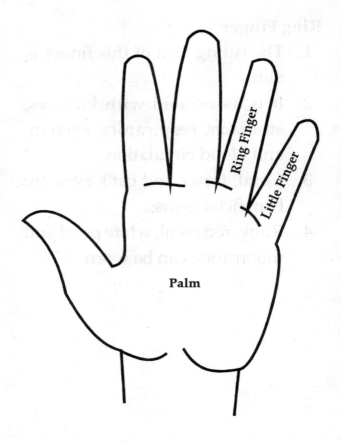

Ring Finger

Little Finger

Palm

Little Finger

1. Mercury governs this finger.
2. It is directly related to the genitals, knees, legs and feet.
3. Sapphire and zircon are the recommended stones.
4. Lapis-lazuli can also be used.

The planets influence our body and certain gems are used for specific planets to counteract the evil effects of malefic planets.

Mars

1. This planet stands for energy, courage, and dare-devilry.
2. A red coral of 9, 11 or 12 gms, set in gold, copper or silver, and worn on the index or ring finger on Tuesday, makes a dull and lethargic person very active and

bright, gives extra-muscular strength, an independent spirit, a strong determination, an ambition for success, and leadership qualities.

3. The ring should be made when Mars is in Capricorn (its exalted sign) and also in Aries.

4. Other benefits that accrue are success in exam, marriage of one's daughter, and procurement of a new job.

5. The diseases that can come from an afflicted Mars are acute fever, plague, measles, smallpox, chickenpox, burns, fistula, wounds, brain fever, typhoid,

haemorrhage, ulcer of the intestines, hernia, malaria, risk of abortions, boils, appendicitis and rheumatism.

Mercury

1. This planet reflects one's intelligence and wisdom.
2. An emerald of 3, 5, 7 or 10 gms, fitted in gold and worn on the little finger on Wednesday, will work wonders for success in exams and competitions.

3. The ring should be made when Mercury is in Virgo.
4. The use of red coral, red cloth, red thread and number nine will help to tap the magical influence of Mars.
5. The diseases related to this planet are vertigo, lethargy, tuberculosis, insanity, dry cough, gout, stammering, leprosy, cancer, skin and stomach diseases.

Venus

1. This planet stands for considerable power and pleasure.

2. This planet governs the gentle and refined attributes, eyes, reproductive system, throat, chin, cheeks and kidneys.

3. If a diamond of 1/4 or 1/2 gms is fitted in a platinum or gold ring, and worn on the middle finger on Friday, great pleasures, comforts and wealth are assured.

4. The ring should be made when Venus is exalted in Pisces, and is positioned in Taurus.

5. An afflicted Venus shows delayed marriage and a disturbed marital life.

Jupiter

2️⃣

1. This is a planet of success.
2. It signifies children and wealth, governs the higher attributes of the mind, and helps in the upliftment of the soul.
3. It rules over the liver, bloodstream, and fat.

4. A yellow sapphire of 7 or 13 gms, set in tin or gold, and worn on the little finger on Thursday, ensures success in every field.

5. The ideal time for making the ring is when Jupiter is positioned in Cancer.

6. The diseases that an afflicted Jupiter can give jaundice, dyspepsia, abscess, pancreas and liver ailments, cerebral congestion, catarrh, carbuncles and flatulence.

Sun

1. It is the significator for royalty, and is a symbol of spirit.

2. A ruby of 3 or 5 gms set in gold and worn on the ring finger on Sundays, will make one determined, self-willed, decisive, cheerful, active authoritative, ambitious, optimistic, brilliant, successful and blessed with sterling qualities.

3. Sun rules the heart, and represents the right eye in men and the left eye in women, mouth, spleen, throat and brain.

4. Diseases accruing from the Sun being afflicted by malefic planets are high blood pressure, haemorrhage, meningitis, loss of speech, typhoid, epilepsy, cardiac thrombosis, eruption on the face, high fevers, and bile complaints.

Moon

1. This planet is the life-giver and life-saver, and represents mind and mother.

2. A white pearl of 2, 4, 6 or 9 gms, fitted in silver, and worn on the little finger on Monday, ensures health, cheer, honour, safe journeys, increase in wealth and pleasantness.

3. This ring should be made when Moon is aspected by Jupiter in Taurus.

4. The diseases related to the moon are eye complaints, lunacy, paralysis, hysteria, epilepsy, beri-beri, cold and cough, colitis, intestinal disorders, tumours, peritoitis, throat problems, asthma, varicose veins, alcoholic

addiction, dyspepsia, dysentery, cancer and typhoid.

Saturn

♄

1. This planet stands for perfection and sophistication.
2. A blue sapphire of 5 or 7 gms, fitted in lead or silver and worn on the middle finger on Saturday, benefits one towards perfection, success in higher studies, and research work.

3. The ring is to be made when Saturn is in Libra (its exalted sign).
4. A black cloth, a black thread, a black pearl and number eight taps the magical force of Saturn.
5. The diseases related to it are jaundice, gout, insanity, leprosy, colitis, paralysis, frequent colds, deafness, and dumbness.

Rahu

1. This planet stands for good health and happiness.

2. A zircon of 6, 11 or 13 gms set in silver and worn on Saturday on the middle finger, gives one peace of mind.

3. It gives wealth and all-round prosperity.

4. It increases one's appetite and vitality.

5. The diseases are cholera, rheumatism, dysentery, and suicidal tendencies.

Ketu

1. This planet ensures life to a dead business.

2. A cat's eye fitted in a steel or gold ring will bestow great

power and strength to the wearer.

3. The ideal time to make the ring will be when Ketu is in Sagittarius.

The Magnetic Power of Gems

1. Gems are mostly used for curative purpose.
2. They are also used for increasing wealth, longevity, power and popularity.
3. The gems, coming in contact with the body, inject rays into the body, restoring the balance between deficiency and excess.
4. Each gem has an abundant source of one specific ray.

Ruby

1. Ruby symbolises the heart of spiritual love and devotion through the forces of purification.
2. It is also an aspect of divine fire and purification.
3. Its fire inspires the love of truth and wisdom.
4. It gives positive life-force qualities.
5. It activates and vitalises the whole body through the circulation of the bloodstream.
6. It has a stimulating vibration.

7. This is useful for the development of soul force and will-power.

8. It cures fever, rheumatism, peptic ulcer, and gout.

9. It brings in a lot of wealth.

10. The individual will always triumph, and lead a royal life.

11. It protects one from fear, afflictions, sorrow and disasters.

12. If the stone is dull, the person's brother might be in distress.

13. A milky stone denotes destruction of cattle.

14. A smoky stone attracts lightning.

15. A dusty-coloured stone causes disorders.

16. White, black or honey-coloured sprinkling on the stone suggest defamation, and decrease in longevity, wealth and comforts.

17. A fading colour signifies some distress or disaster.

18. A depression in the stone means ill-health, and loss of stamina and vitality.

Pearl

1. Pale and luminescent, pearls are connected with the moon and feminine, mystical qualities

often symbolised by water, secrets, and wisdom.

2. Pearls also symbolise longevity as well as patience, tranquillity, and purity.

3. It strengthens the mind force.

4. It helps us reach a higher level through the practice of sacrifice and devotional love.

5. Its high calcium content contains curative properties.

6. It helps to cure insomnia, uterine disorders, heart and eye problems, tuberculosis, hysteria and pleurisy.

7. It controls one's rash temper, and makes conjugal life

harmonious, removes depression, inspires love and faithfulness, and bestows one with a good memory.

8. It increases one's good fortune, fame, wealth, longevity and popularity.

9. A pearl with a yellow lustre ensures wealth.

10. The red-coloured variety makes one intelligent.

11. A white pearl bestows fame.

12. A blue one brings in good fortune.

13. A spotted pearl causes leprosy.

14. A fish-eyed sign on a pearl suggest loss of children.

15. A lustreless pearl shortens one's life.
16. A pearl resembling a coral invites poverty.
17. A broken pearl spells loss of livelihood.

Coral
1. This symbolises life-force energy.
2. It protects one from the evil eye.
3. The dark red variety vitatises and stimulates the bloodstream and the entire body.
4. The pink variety restores harmony where there is a conflict of emotion.

5. It aids during meditation by helping one to retain images and forms.

6. It blesses one with material happiness.

7. It helps one to recover from fever, cough, smallpox, chickenpox, headache, piles, measles and bilious complaints.

8. It frees one from nightmares and unpleasant dreams.

9. It makes one courageous and triumphant.

10. The red coral warns one of impending ill-health by changing its colour.

Emerald

1. The lush and intense green colour of the emerald is associated with fertility and life.
2. It is also associated with wisdom and faith.
3. The emerald instils divine qualities through the power and beauty of its ray.
4. It is a symbol of regeneration and life. It represents a revitalised body in which the higher soul flowers with creative and artistic abilities.
5. While energising and replenishing, it is also restful and calming.

6. Its rays help in balancing, healing and providing one with a serene state of mind.
7. This increases one's intelligence, brain power and wisdom.
8. The clear shades of emerald are good for meditation.
9. Writers might consider adopting emeralds as their personal gem, since it is linked with powers of persuasion and verbal eloquence.
10. Emeralds are associated with the preservation of chastity.
11. They are effective in countering evil spirits.

12. It is a sure cure for stammering, fear, amnesia, epilepsy, fickle-mindedness, ulcer, diarrhoea, dysentery, gastritis, asthma, heart problems and insomnia.

13. It ensures wealth, property and offsprings.

14. It protects one from evil influences and snake bites.

15. A flawed stone may cause injuries, and deprive them of happiness from parents.

Topaz

1. Topaz has an inspiring and stimulating influence on the higher mind and soul.

2. It sharpens one's awareness and vision.
3. It endows one with a great capability of keenness, clarity, concentration and creativity.
4. It has a balancing effect on the nervous system and on the solar plexus.
5. It is an excellent aid in cases of nervous trauma, exhaustion or mental breakdown.
6. It increases wealth, prosperity and life security.
7. It dispels adversity, misfortune and melancholia.
8. It cures diarrhoea, gastritis, ulcer, heart problems, rheuma-

tism, jaundice, insomnia, impotency, gout and arthritis.

Diamond

1. Diamonds symbolise our deepest love, and honour our most lasting commitments.
2. The diamond is the highest expression of white light — the universal light.
3. It is the highest symbol of clarity, purity and illumination, and represents the pure focus of energy.
4. It harmonises the heart and the will with divine mind, creating perfection.

5. It is the gem with the highest potency.
6. It carries great healing power, curing most illneses.
7. It protects against negative vibrations and thoughts.
8. Its pure transparency and reflection cut through all, yet nothing cuts through it.
9. It creates goodness and goodwill.
10. It expels evil and fearful thoughts.
11. It improves the financial status and peace of mind.
12. It cures diabetes, afflicted genitals, skin and uterine disorders.

13. It protects one from the influence of evil spirits and snake-bites.

14. A diamond with a red hue is beneficial to kings, administrators and political leaders.

15. A stone with a white hue benefits those associated with religious and spiritual work.

16. A black-hued one helps those in inferior or menial tasks.

17. A defective diamond brings disaster and distress, and disturbs one's peace of mind.

Sapphire

1. It ensure a long, energetic life.

2. It promises wealth, name and fame, joy, love and happiness to the wearer.

3. It cures deafness, baldness, mental disorders, infertility, fainting fits and virility.

4. The wearer of this gem will be blessed with children and grandchildren, and will be protected from evil sprits.

5. A stone with cracks denotes accidents.

6. A lustreless and opaque stone causes distress to near ones.

7. A milky stone suggests poverty.

8. A double-coloured stone causes trouble from enemies.

9. A red-dotted stone denotes loss of wealth.
10. A stone with a depression signifies problems from boils and ulcers.

Zircon

1. This gem confers success and prosperity.
2. It ensures good appetite, vitality and good health.
3. It brings wealth, prosperity and happiness to the individual.
4. It safeguards one from enemies and criticism.
5. The red-hued stone is injurious to health.

Cat's Eye

1. Gains profit from speculations, gambling, horse racing, and stocks shares.
2. It cures paralysis and mania.
3. It saves one from unexpected mishaps, secret enemies and poverty.
4. It bestows wealth and children to the wearer of the gem.
5. It restores lost health.
6. A dull or opaque stone is not good for health.
7. A spotted stone means trouble from enemies.
8. The one with a depression causes stomach ailments.

9. A cracked stone warns of injuries.
10. A webbed stone denotes imprisonment.
11. A black-spotted stone is fatal to the subject.

Composition of Gems

Various gems are in constant use, but of these, nine are claimed to be superior while eighteen of them are of lesser relevance.

Ruby

1. This is a gem of various shades of red corundum.
2. Some stones are pink, some blackish and some pale-coloured.
3. It is a hot stone, and one of the most valued among precious stones.

4. It generally occurs in crystals of six-sided prisms.

5. All are translucent and suitable due to their wide range of colour, and hardness.

6. A flawless ruby is smooth, having a lustre, brilliance and radiance, and a rich, red colour.

7. Rubies are very costly because of their scarcity.

8. A large ruby is more rare and more expensive than a large diamond.

9. The best ruby is the one which, when immersed in milk, emits red rays in the milk, or the one

whose rays are red in the early morning sun, or it glows in darkness.

10. The rarest and most expensive shade is described as being the colour of pigeon's blood — a rich, velvety, deep red, but without fire or sparkle.

11. Because rubies are more opaque than diamonds and lack sparkle and brilliance, they are cut differently.

12. The stone is polished and cut into a convex form, but is not faceted. This is most commonly used for rubies because it

accentuates the colour of the gem.

13. A blemished ruby has a depression, or a pale tinge of colour, or else has sprinklings of white, black or honey-coloured dots.

14. The deepening colour of ruby with time is an indication of grave danger and great personal misfortune.

Diamond

1. This is a mineral, one of the two crystalline forms of the element carbon — the drab-sounding dark substance behind the

world's most dazzling jewel —, and the hardest known substance used as a gem.

2. It is a hot gem of white, yellow, red, pink, blue, green or black colour.

3. Unlike other gems, diamonds are prized for their absence of colour. The clearer the stone, the more valuable the diamond.

4. The diamond that is colourless, with a tinge of blue or sprays of blue and red rays, is considered to be the best, and the most common variety used in jewellery.

5. A coloured stone is called a "fancy diamond".

6. Clarity refers to imperfections in the stone. A diamond free of any imperfections visible under a ten-power microscope is considered flawless.

7. A diamond is blemished if it has dots or has the impression of a drop of water.

8. Its specific gravity is remarkably constant, the refractive index is the highest among all gemstones, and the dispersion is very strong.

9. A hexagonal or octagonal diamond, if reflected on water,

displays the seven colours of the rainbow.

10. As for carats, a two-carat diamond can easily cost more than twice as much as a one-carat diamond.

11. The cut of a diamond is the "C" that carries the most clout because cutting determines the diamond's beauty and brilliance. Cutting is the spark that ignites the fire of the stone, by luring light into the gem that's then reflected back out as sparkling brilliance.

12. The size of the diamond is not nearly as important as the cut; a

big stone is less valuable than a masterfully cut smaller one.

13. Diamonds may be cut into round, oval, pear or emerald shapes.

14. Round, the most popular cut, is called "brilliant" because it creates the most light.

15. The oval, pear-shaped or emerald-shaped cuts can actually make diamonds appear larger than they are.

Pearl

1. Pearl is obtained from certain shelled molluscs, chiefly the oyster or freshwater mussel.

2. Although organic, the pearl is composed mainly of mineral matter.
3. Cuttured pearls are coveted for jewellery and are created by interfering with the natural process.
4. To the untrained eye, it is impossible to tell the difference between a cultured pearl and a natural one.
5. Natural pearls can be ten times more expensive than their cultured counterparts.
6. Pearls, like most gems, are judged on colour, and form three basic groups — white with

creamy and pink being the most desirable; black and various shades of grey; and coloured pearls, which are almost always of fresh water origin.

7. The best variety is the pink one which is lustrous, clear and heavy, and is the most precious among pearls.

8. The pure pearl is lustrous and round, though the long and the flat ones also have certain curative powers.

9. A blemished pearl is broken, or has spots or cracks, and is dull in colour.

Emerald

1. This gem is a rich variety of beryl, and the colour is due to the presence of chromium oxide.
2. It is a hot stone, and is one of the most expensive gemstones.
3. Its colours range from a deep velvet green to a bright grass green.
4. A flawless emerald is smooth and transparent, and has radiance and brilliance, spraying bright rays.
5. A blemished stone has a depression or cracks, is lustrous but brittle, or has black or yellow spots with a rough surface.

6. They are softer than diamonds, rubies or sapphires.
7. They lack much brilliance and have virtually no fire. Because colour rather than brilliance, makes emeralds valuable the convex cut is how an important emerald is usually crafted.

Coral

1. A coral is the hard, calcareous, red, white or black skeleton of any of the various marine invertebrate animals. These skeletons collectively form reefs or islands.

2. Its colour varies from shades of red to white and yellow.
3. A good and flawless coral will be perfectly round or oval, of an opaque red colour, emitting a sheen, and having a smooth surface.
4. It is smooth, and devoid of any hole or perforation.
5. The blemished coral has black or white spots, a depression, a crack, a bend or a twist on the surface and is sometimes multi-hued.
6. The coral is worn for life and blood force.

Topaz

1. This is a transparent mineral gem, being a silicate and fluoride of aluminium, and generally found in granite rocks.
2. It is a cold gem, occurring naturally in a prismatic form with a pyramidal termination.
3. Its colour is yellow, but it also occurs in pink and blue shades.
4. The blemished stone has cracks, or red dots, or a depression.

Sapphire

1. The blue sapphire is believed to bestow purity of purpose and deed.

2. This is a valuable blue variety of corundum.
3. Sapphires and rubies are actually different colours of the same mineral, corundum. But while rubies are always red, sapphires come in a variety of colours — pink, orange, violet, green, yellow, and of course, blue.
4. It is a cold gem, with the same hardness, specific gravity and refracting indices as those of ruby.
5. The best blue sapphire does not change its colour when held in

front of an electric light, while others show a navy blue tinge.

6. It is smooth and transparent, soft to the touch, and it sends out rays from inside.

7. The star sapphire is the "stone of destiny", in which three crossed lines intersect in the centre of the stone, symbolising faith, destiny and hope.

8. Sapphires are believed to ward off fraud and terror, protecting one from dangers and envy.

9. A blemished stone may have white lines on it, or a depression, or it may be dull and opaque, or else is double-coloured or milky.

Zircon

1. This is a common tetragonal mineral, occurring in small, opaque or transparent prismatic crystals.

2. Resembling a diamond, it is a cold stone.

3. It is naturally colourless, reddish-orange, brownish-red, grey, violet-grey, or green.

4. When heated, it turns bluish-white, and the translucent specimen is used as a gem.

5. A good stone reflects a golden colour when seen from a distance, is transparent and

homogeneous, soft to the touch, lustrous and radiant.

6. A blemished stone shows a light blackish hue from a distance, is dull, flat-bodied, full of layers, or resembles a yellow piece of glass.

Cat's Eye

1. This is a hard, semi-transparent variety of quartz, much valued as a gem.

2. This very hot stone is opalescent, and is of various shades ranging from a cloudy yellow to a brownish-green colour.

3. Due to its opalescent radiation of colours that resemble a cat's eye, it is called so.

4. The pure variety has a yellowish radiance and a white, brilliant straight band.

5. The blemished one has a depression, or spots, webbed lines, or a dull sheen.

The semiprecious stones of lesser reference and used as substitutes are:

1. *Opal*

A mineral consisting of hydrous silica, occurring in numerous varieties and colours, neither as hard nor as dense as quartz, the finest characterised by an iridescent reflection of light. The use of opal lifts ordinary consciousness to cosmic awareness.

2. *Peridot*

A precious stone of yellowish-green colour.

3. *Tourmaline*

A complex soft silicate mineral of boron and aluminium, occurring in black, red, green, brown and white colours, the clear varieties being used as gems.

4. *Amethyst*

The violet variety of quartz is used as a precious stone, containing traces of manganese, titanium and iron.

5. *Rock Crystal*

A transparent quartz of a colourless or a shining white colour.

6. *Moonstone*

A translucent variety of feldspar with a pearly lustre, and having a glistening band inside which rolls with the turn of the stone.

7. *Garnet*

A hard, vitreous silicate mineral occurring in a number of varieties; the common deep red transparent variety are used as gems.

8. *Aquamarine*

The finest beryl, and so called because of its bluish, sea-green, bluish-green tint and it is transparent.

9. *Bloodstone*

A greenish kind of quartz with small blood-like spots of red jasper scattered through it.

10. *Lapis-lazuli*

A soft, semiprecious stone of a rich blue colour, consisting of lazurite and other minerals.

11. *Agate*

A semiprecious pellucid mineral, consisting of bands or layers of various colours blended together.

12. *Turquoise*

A sky-blue or greenish-blue mineral. It is worn for protection and is believed to purify the atmosphere of the world.

13. *Jade*

    A hard gemstone, either nephritic or jadeite, often green in colour, either translucent or opaque, and sometimes veined.

14. *Gypsum*

    A mineral, a hydrous sulphate of calcium, occurring both in crystalline and massive forms.

15. *Smoky quartz*

    A variety of crystallised quartz, ranging in colour from light yellow to deep brown.

16. *Onyx*

    A semi-pellucid, dark green stone with variously coloured veins.

17. *Carnelian*

    A variety of chalcedony, of a deep red, flesh-red, or pale reddish colour.

18. *Jasper*

    An opaque, dark red quartz, which takes on an elegant polish.

Gems and Diseases

Acidosis

1. This occurs due to excessive production of acid in the body.
2. The symptoms are headache, rapid breathing, debility, and a sweetish odour to the breath.

Curative Measures :

An emerald of 5 gms on the middle finger, a yellow sapphire of 5 gms on the ring finger will be beneficial.

In acute cases, a moonstone of 6 gms on the index finger is recommended

Accidents

1. Accidents means cut, injuries and bloodshed.

Curative Measures :

Red coral or white pearl is beneficial.

Acne

1. Eruption of pimples on the skin is known as acne.
2. The affected areas could be the nose, cheeks, forehead and chin.

Curative Measures :

A white coral of 7 or 9 gms on the middle finger, and a lapis-lazuli of 2gms on the little finger are recommended.

Allergy

1. Some drugs or chemicals cause allergy in certain people.
2. The digestive system, skin, bronchi and nose are mainly affected.
3. The common types of allergic disorders are bronchial asthma, eczema, hay fever, rashes and headaches.

Curative Measures :

Cold stones like yellow sapphire, moonstone, blue sapphire and emerald are the recommended stones.

Ague

1. Chills and fevers from malaria are know as ague.
2. Metallic fumes and poisonous intakes can also cause ague.

Curative Measures :

Red coral of 7 to 8 gms worn on the ring finger, or a copper ring, a red thread or a cloth around the working hand will cure one of this ailment.

Amenorrhoea

1. Ceasing of menstruation or a missed period due to pregnancy or hormonal imbalance is known as amenorrhoea.

2. Temporary amenorrhoea can also be caused by excessive fatigue and anxiety.

Curative Measures :

Red coral or copper ring, red cloth or thread on the left hand will counteract the disease.

Adenoids

1. This is the enlargement of the lymphoid tissue in the throat and at the back of the nose.
2. The symptoms are blockage of the nasal passage, colds, sinus infection and ear infections.

Curative Measures :

Red coral of 5 gms worn on the ring finger will be beneficial.

Amnesia

1. This is a partial or total loss of memory.
2. This is due to changes in the tissues of the brain.

Curative Measures :

Red coral of 7 to 9 gms and an emerald of 6 gms should be used.

Anaemia

1. This is due to drastic reduction of red corpuscles in the blood.

2. This results from loss of blood through haemorrhage, or through disorders of the bone marrow.

Curative Measures :
Use coral of 7 to 9 gms, or yellow sapphire of 5 gms.

Apoplexy

1. Also known as cerebral haemorrhage, this causes rupture of a blood vessel and leads to a stroke.

2. The patient becomes unconscious and then paralysis sets in.

Curative Measures :

Red coral of 7 to 9 gms, and yellow sapphire of 5 gms, should be used.

Appendicitis

1. A small finger-like projection by the large intestine gets inflamed, causing severe pain.

Curative Measures :

Red coral and yellow sapphire will help in dissolving the inflammation.

Arthritis

1. Inflammation of joints due to deposits of crystallised uric acid

in the cartilages results in arthritis.

2. Reduction of body weight, intake of less protein rich foods, and acupuncture are measures to be adopted by arresting arthritis.

Curative Measures :

Red coral of 9 gms and yellow sapphire of 5 gms are recommended for use.

Asthma

1. Secretion of excess mucous, and the narrowing of bronchial tubes by spasmodic contractions causes asthma.

2. Wheezing, coughing and laborious breathing make a patient suffer.

Curative Measures :

Emerald of 6 gms and yellow sapphire of 5 gms are recommended.

In acute cases a moonstone of 6 gms, can also be used as an additional gem.

Atrophy

1. This disease occurs due to the degeneration of body tissues.

2. This disease may affect any part of the body, whereby the flesh, tissue, cell or organ wastes away.

Curative Measures :

Red coral of 9 gms and yellow sapphire of 5 gms are recommended.

Backache

1. This can be caused by standing or sitting in a peculiar position all day long, by straining, sudden jerking, lifting of weight or deep-seated mental stress.

Curative Measures :

Red coral of 9 gms and yellow sapphire of 5 gms are recommended.

Baldness

1. This is hereditary, and beyond cure.

Curative Measures :

The combined use of blue sapphire and emerald will give life to the hair-roots.

Biliousness

1. It is caused by an excess bile secretion of bile in the liver.

Curative Measures :

Blue sapphire and emerald, or moonstone and white coral can be used.

Bladder Disorders

1. This is indicated by difficulty in passing urine.
2. This could be due to serious kidney trouble or enlarged prostrate glands.

Curative Measures :

Red coral of 9 gms and yellow sapphire of 5 gms, or white coral of 9 gms moonstone should be used.

Bleeding Wounds

1. This is caused by cuts, wounds and accidents.
2. Bleeding from mouth, nose, nipples, anus and

ears is dangerous and needs prompt attention.

Curative Measures :

Red coral cures this.

Blindness

1. Infections, diseases related to the eye or an accident may cause blindness — temporary or permanent.

Curative Measures :

Ruby and white pearl may be useful for temporary or partial blindness.

Blisters

1. This is due to accumulation of fluid under the skin.
2. This is caused by fevers, burns, chemicals or acids.

Curative Measures :

Red coral, red cloth, red thread or a copper ring are recommended as a supplement to medicines.

Boils

1. These can be in the form of pimples or carbuncles.
2. Diabetics and those with kidney problems are prone to boils.

Curative Measures :

Moonstone of 6 gms or lapis-
lazuli of 4 gms should be used.

Bone Diseases

1. Osteomyelitis is inflammation
   of the bone, commonly affecting
   the hip and shin bones.
2. Osteitis is bone inflammation
   caused by overactivity of the
   parathyroid gland.
3. Syphilis destroys the bone ends
   where they meet in joints, being
   very brittle.

Curative Measures :

During winter months, a red
cloth or thread, a copper ring or
red coral should be used.

In summer, lapis-lazuli, a black cloth or thread, or a steel ring will be beneficial.

Brain Tumours

1. This is caused by growth of new and unwanted tissues in the brain.
2. Headache, dizziness, uncontrolled vomiting are the common symptoms.
3. If timely attention is not given, it could lead to blindness, insanity, and non-functional sensory organs.

Curative Measures :

Emerald, yellow sapphire and red coral are recommended.

Bronchitis

1. Inflammation of the bronchial tubes cause this lung disease.
2. Fumes, dust, exposure to cold and inhalation of irritating gases lead to this problem, due to which cold, fever and also a dry cough, result.

Curative Measures :

Red coral of 7 to 9 gms set in a ring and worn on the ring finger will be a good supplement to medicines.

Burns

1. Burns may result from overheat or fire to the skin.

2. Scalding results from hot liquids or vapours on the skin.
3. First-degree burns show redness of the skin, second degree, shows skin blisters and some breaking of the skin. In the third degree, destruction of the skin and its underlying tissues and in the fourth degree, charring and blackening occur.

Curative Measures :

Red coral of 9 gms, a red cloth or thread may help in quick healing when supplemented by first aid and medicines.

Cancer

1. This is a tumour or unwanted growth of body cells, which can be benign or malignant.
2. Carcinoma is cancer of the skin, glands or membranes, sarcoma is of the bone, leukaemia is of the blood, while melannia is of the pigment cells of the skin.
3. It is neither contagious, communicable, nor hereditary.
4. The symptoms are sores that do not heal, particularly in the mouth, lips or tongue, a lump, bleeding from an opening, persistent

hoarseness and indigestion, difficulty in swallowing, change in bowel movements and colour or size of a mole or wart.

Curative Measures :

A light blue sapphire worn on the middle finger shows remarkable recovery, and a red coral ring on the ring finger should also be worn.

Cataract

1. The crystalline lens of the eye becomes opaque, and one's vision becomes poor.

Curative Measures :

Red coral and white pearl are the ideal gems for the cure of cataract.

Emerald as an additional stone should be used in acute cases.

Cerebral Haemorrhage

1. Bleeding in the brain results in a stroke or apoplexy.
2. Symptoms are unconsciousness and paralysis.

Curative Measures :

Red coral, emerald and moonstone are the recommended gems for its cure.

Chelitis

1. This is an inflammation of the lips and the corners of the mouth.
2. Its causes are sunburn, lipstick or chemical irritants.

Curative Measures :

Red coral, a red cloth or thread, or a copper ring works wonders.

Chickenpox

1. It is caused by virus.
2. The symptoms are slight fever and discomfort, and eruptions on the skin, starting from the face.

3. It is a contagious disease, and offers immunity after one attack.

Curative Measures :

Red coral, a red cloth or thread, or a copper coin is used to mitigate the effect.

Cholera

1. It is caused by an organism called vibrio cholera.
2. It is contagious.
3. The symptoms are sudden onset of explosive diarrhoea, leading to profound dehydration within hours, slight fever, and sometimes vomiting.

Curative Measures :

Emerald of 6 gms and yellow sapphire or moonstone are recommended.

Cirrhosis of the Liver

1. Severe damage to the cells of the liver due to excessive drinking leads to progressive liver failure.

2. Alcohol, viral hepatitis and certain forms of gall bladder and biliary disease are the main causes.

3. The symptoms start with loss of appetite, fatigue, weakness and weight loss, followed by

nausea, vomiting, abdominal
discomfort and anaemia.
4. Acute cases lead to jaundice and
coma.

Curative Measures :
Emerald and yellow sapphire,
with moonstone of 6 gms as an
additional gem for acute cases,
are recommended.

Colitis
1. This is an inflammation of the
intestines accompanied by
severe pain.
2. In the chronic form of ulcerative
colitis, severe diarrhoea results,
which can be recurring and fatal.

3. Food poisoning and overdose of certain antibiotics may upset the bowels.

Curative Measures :
Emerald and moonstone should cure it.

Colour Blindness

1. A hereditary disease, where the patient is unable to distinguish between red and green.

Curative Measures :
Red coral and white pearl should help.

Common Cold

1. An infectious disease of the respiratory system, particularly the nose, throat and bronchi, caused by a large number of viruses.

2. The symptoms are a stuffy or running nose, headache and cough, with a feeling of chilliness, and sometimes a slight fever.

Curative Measures :

Red coral of 7 to 9 gms, or a red cloth or thread, or a copper ring will help.

Conjunctivitis

1. This is an inflammation of the membrane of the eyes, noticed as redness and irritation of the white parts of the eye.
2. It is highly contagious.

Curative Measures:

Moonstone of 6 gms is recommended.

Constipation

1. This is an unexplained delay and difficulty passing of stools.

Curative Measures:

Red coral, red cloth or thread, or a copper ring will provide relief.

Cramps

1. This is a sudden, involuntary, persistent contraction of a muscle or muscles.
2. Cramps may manifest during menstruation, swimming or any sports activity, or writing.

Curative Measures :

Red coral, a red cloth or thread, or a copper ring are useful.

Croup

1. This is acute inflammation and swelling of the area in the vocal cords, causing a harsh, rasping sound while breathing.

2. Generally, it affects babies and children up to three years of age.

Curative Measures :

Red coral is beneficial.

Deafness

1. There is a partial or total loss of hearing due to mechanical failure, nerve damage or brain transmission problems.

Curative Measures :

Red coral of 9 gms, and emerald of 5 gms worn on the middle finger in acute cases, are recommended.

Dermatitis

1. This is a chronic skin inflammation localised to one area of the body.

2. The symptoms are dry, very itchy and scaly patch of skin that becomes thickened and pigmented.

Curative Measures :

White coral of 7 to 9 gms and lapis- lazuli of 3 gms are best.

Diabetes Mellitus

1. This is a disease in which the body is unable to correctly metabolise glucose for energy.

2. The symptoms are immense thirst, increased urine output, fatigue, blurred vision, increased appetite and weight loss.

Curative Measures :

Red coral and yellow sapphire, or red coral and lapis-lazuli set in pure silver are recommended.

Diarrhoea

1. The general symptoms are loose or frequent bowel movements accompanied by stomach-ache.

Curative Measures :

Emeralds and yellow sapphire or moonstone are beneficial.

Dribbling

1. This is the inability to withhold the flow of urine, due to bladder or kidney trouble.

Curative Measures :

White or red coral should be used.

Dropsy

1. This results from excessive accumulation of fluid in the body tissues, due to heart disorders, blood vessels or kidneys.

2. The common symptoms are swollen ankles and abdomen.

Curative Measures :

Red coral and yellow sapphire are useful.

Dysentery

1. This is infection of the bowed caused by amoebae or shigella bacteria.

2. The symptoms are acute diarrhoea with mucus and blood, mild fever and abdominal cramps, leading to severe weakness and dehydration.

Curative Measures :

Emerald and yellow sapphire or moonstone are best.

Dysmenorrhoea

1. This is painful menstruation caused by hormonal imbalance, uterine tumour, fibroid tumours or pelvic inflammatory disease.

Curative Measures :

White and red coral on the middle finger will give relief.

Eczema

1. This is inflammation, itching and scaliness of the skin, caused by toxic irritants.

Curative Measures :

White coral and yellow sapphire are useful.

Enuresis

1. It is involuntary discharge of urine while sleeping also called bed-wetting.

Curative Measures :

Red coral and emerald should be used.

Epilepsy

1. Sudden disturbance of the brain function can lead to violent fits or convulsions, resulting in temporary loss of consciousness.

Curative Measures :

Emerald, moonstone, and also red coral, may be used.

Fistula

1. This is an abnormal passage connecting two hollow organs.
2. It may develop from a fissure, an abscess, an operation scar or sonal abnormal condition in a tissue.

Curative Measures :

The condition may be extremely sensitive and painful.

Gallstones

1. This is a solid, pebble-like mass formed in the gall bladder.
2. The symptoms are pain, nausea, vomiting, slight fever and chronic indigestion.

Curative Measures :

Red coral and emerald are useful, while yellow sapphire or moonstone may be used as additional also in acute cases.

Gangrene

1. This is the death of tissues caused by lack of oxygen in the cells, usually the result of the blood supply being cut off.

2. This may occur due to frostbite and severe wounds which don't get immediate medical care, leading to coldness and numbness, and then it turns black, painful and swollen.

Curative Measures :

Emerald and yellow sapphire on the middle or ring finger respectively, with moonstone in acute cases, may be used.

Glandular Fever

1. An excessive increase in the number of white corpuscles in the bloodstream leads to high fever, with the lymph glands inflamed.

Curative Measures :

Red coral, a red cloth or thread, may be used.

Glaucoma

1. This is a disorder of the eyes caused by increased pressure of fluids within the eyeballs, which may lead to blindness if not attended to immediately.

Curative Measures :

Red coral and white pearl are suggested.

Gonorrhoea

1. This is a venereal disease caused by a bacterium contacted during sexual intercourse.
2. The symptoms are burning and pain during urination, and

discharge of a few drops of pus from the penis.

Curative Measures :

Red coral of 9 gms and moonstone are best.

Gout

1. This is a disease in which the chemical processes in the body are upset, leading to the production of abnormally large amounts of uric acid.
2. In an acute attack, a joint becomes hot, swollen, red, very tender and painful.
3. In chronic cases, it can lead to severe deformities of the hands and feet.

Curative Measures :

Red coral or yellow sapphire is recommended.

Hay Fever

1. This is an inflammation inside the nose due to an allergy.
2. The symptoms resemble those of a common cold, accompanied by fever.

Curative Measures :

Red coral and emerald are suggested.

Headache

1. The blood vessels in the brain are interlaced with many nerves,

and it is in these nerves that the pain of a headache originates.

2. Headaches can be in the form of tension headaches or migraines, and can be caused by eyestrain, sinusitis, common cold, influenza, allergies, menstrua-tion, high blood pressure, injuries to the head or spine, brain tumour, hunger, cold, lack of sleep, fatigue or too much drinking or smoking.

Curative Measures :

Emerald and moonstone should be used.

Hepatitis

1. This is inflammation of the **liver,** generally caused by a virus.
2. Emerald and yellow sapphire, with moonstone as **an** additional gem, are recommended.

Hernia

1. A weakening of the **tissue,** generally muscle, surrounding an organ, leads to a portion of the organ bulging through the weak point.

Curative Measures :

Red coral and yellow sapphire are useful for this.

Hydrocele

1. There is an accumulation of fluid in the scrotal sac, causing it to swell.

Curative Measures :

Red coral and moonstone are recommended.

Hysteria

1. This is a condition in which symptoms are usually seen in disease produced by the unconscious action of the mind.
2. The symptoms may be in the form of dumbness, deafness, blindness, paralysis, loss of memory, fainting spells and neurosis.

Curative Measures:

Red coral and moonstone are best.

Impotence

1. This is the inability of a man to complete sexual intercourse.
2. This may be caused by nerve injuries, excessive indulgence in sexual activities early in life, or alcoholic addiction.

Curative Measures:

Red and white coral, with yellow sapphire as an additional gem, are suggested.

Influenza

1. This is an acute disease caused by a virus, in which the symptoms include chills and fever, headache, loss of appetite, aches and pains, weakness, and inflammation of the mucous membrane.

Curative Measures:

Red coral and yellow sapphire are best.

Insanity

1. This is a mental disease, verging on madness, whereby temporary distortions of the mental frame, like loss of

memory or concentration, frequently occur.

Curative Measures :

Emerald, red coral and moonstone can be used.

Insomnia

1. This is the inability to fall asleep or to sleep restfully. It is due to excessive fatigue, heavy and rich meals, caffeine, fear or anxiety.

Curative Measures :

Emerald, moonstone and yellow sapphire are best.

Jaundice

1. This is caused by an excessive secretion of bilirubin, a constituent of the bile.

2. This could be due to excessive breakdown of red blood cells, or when the liver cells are unable to deal with the bile in the normal way, or due to a gallstone in the gall bladder.

Curative Measures :

Deep red coral of 7 to 8 gms on the right arm worn with a red thread, and very light blue sapphire of 5 gms on the middle finger will give complete relief.

Kalaazar

1. This is a parasitic disease of the liver and spleen, causing enlargement of the organs, progressive anaemia, intermittent fever, and swollen legs.

Curative Measures :

Red coral and moonstone, with emeralds as an additional stone, are used.

Laryngitis

1. This is an inflammation of the voice box, causing hoarseness, soreness and wheezy breathing, and a ticklish feeling in the throat.

Curative Measures :

Red coral is best.

Leprosy

1. This is an infectious disease of the skin, nerves muscles and bones, causing discoloured patches on the skin with loss of sensation there, numbness in the hands and feet.

Curative Measures :

Zircon and red coral or white coral may be useful.

Leucoderma

1. This is a condition in which there is an absence of the dark

pigment, melanin, white patches appear on the skin, but is harmless.

Curative Measures :

Light blue sapphire of 5 gms and diamond of 1/2 gm on the middle finger are essential.

Leukaemia

1. This is a disease in which there is an abnormally large number of white blood cells in the blood, and blood-forming tissues, and can be cancerous.

Curative Measures :

Red coral and zircon or cat's eye, yellow sapphire and zircon are recommended.

Malaria

1. This is a disease caused by a microscopic parasite transmitted by the bites of anopheles mosquitoes.
2. It is marked by acute attacks of chills and high fever, headaches, anaemia, and muscular pains.

Curative Measures :

Red coral and moonstone are advised to be used.

Measles

1. This is a contagious disease caused by a virus, causing pink rashes on the face, neck and body accompanied with, sore

eyes, sneezing, coughing, running nose and fever.

Curative Measures :

Red coral, or a red cloth or thread, or a copper ring are beneficial.

Meningitis

1. This is the inflammation of the membranes covering the brain and spinal cord, caused by a bacterium.

2. The symptoms are severe headache, high fever, vomiting, and often stiffness of neck and back muscles.

Curative Measures :

Emerald, yellow sapphire and red coral should be used.

Menstrual Disorders

1. Hormonal disorders are amenorrhoeas excessive and prolonged menstruation, irregular menstruation, or menopause.

Curative Measures :

White pearl of 10 to 12 gms, and red coral as an additional gem, are recommended.

Mumps

1. This is an acute, contagious disease caused by a virus and

transmitted in the saliva of an infected person.

2. Swelling of the face and neck, an inflamed parotoid gland, headache and fever are common symptoms.

Curative Measures :
Red or white coral is ideal for treatment.

Myopia

1. This is the ability to see distinctly only things that are close, also called short-sightedness.

Curative Measures :

Red coral and white pearl
should cure one.

Neuralgia

1. This is a severe pain along the
   course of a nerve, caused by an
   injury or an irritation.

Curative Measures :

Red coral and emerald are
recommended.

Neuritis

1. This is an inflammation of a
   nerve or nerves of the peripheral
   nervous system, causing pain
   along the course of the vein.

Curative Measures :

Red coral and emerald relieves one of this condition.

Osteitis

1. This is an inflammation of the bones, caused by overactivity of the parathyroid glands.

Curative Measures :

Red coral and moonstone are ideal gems.

Paralysis

1. This is partial or complete loss of sensation in part or parts of the body, caused by disease or injury to some portion of the nervous system.

Curative Measures :

Red coral and emerald, with moonstone as an additional gem, are recommended.

Piles

1. This is an enlarged vein in the wall of the ano-rectal canal, bringing discomfort or severe pain, often causing bleeding.

Curative Measures :

Red or white coral with moonstone are advised.

Pleurisy

1. This is an inflammation of the pleura, the double membrane

that covers each lung and lines the chest cavity.

2. The common symptoms are sharp pains in the lungs, chills, fever, dry cough and difficult breathing.

Curative Measures :
Red coral and yellow sapphire would be best.

Pneumonia

1. This is an acute inflammation of the lungs, in which the tiny air sacs become so filled up with fluid that breathing is affected.

Curative Measures :

Red coral and yellow sapphire are recommended.

Poliomyelitis

1. This is an acute infection of the nervous system, sometimes resulting in paralysis, caused by a virus.

2. The symptoms are fever, headaches, vomiting, drowsiness, and stiffness in the neck and back.

Curative Measures :

Blue sapphire and red coral are ideal gems for this.

Rheumatism

1. This involves pain in the joints and bones, and the tissues supporting them.

Curative Measures :

Red coral and yellow sapphire are recommended.

Smallpox

1. This is a highly contagious viral disease characterised by a rash that leaves pitted scars on the skin.

2. Fever, headache, nausea and pinkish-red spots are the general symptoms.

Curative Measures :

Red coral, or a red cloth or thread and a copper ring are recommended.

Sunstroke

1. This is caused by excessive exposure to the sun, leading to headache, weakness and dizziness, followed by fever.

Curative Measures :

Yellow sapphire is ideal.

Syphilis

1. This is a venereal disease caused by a germ and transmitted by sexual contact.

Curative Measures :

Red and white coral are suitable.

Toothache

1. The most frequent cause of toothache is decay of the tooth, others being an abscess, abnormal pressure from an incorrect bite, an impacted wisdom tooth, or neuralgia in a facial nerve.

Curative Measures :

Red or white coral should help.

Tuberculosis

1. This is an infectious, communicable disease, caused by a bacterium.

2. This may affect the lungs, larynx, bones and joints, skin, lymph nodes, intestines, kidneys, and the nervous system.

Curative Measures :

Red coral and yellow sapphire, with white pearl as an additional gem, are used.

Typhoid Fever

1. A serious infectious disease caused by a bacterium, transmitted by contaminated water, milk and other foods.
2. The symptoms are headache, high fever, red spots on chest

and abdomen, and chills and sweating.

Curative Measures :

Emerald, yellow sapphire and moonstone are recommended for use.

Whooping Cough

1. An acute, very contagious disease of the bronchial tubes and the upper respiratory passages, primarily in childhood.
2. The symptoms are a severe cold, fever and a persistent whoop kind of cough.

Curative Measures :

Red coral, red cloth or thread, and a copper ring are beneficial.